Shakespeare Road SERIES

A Work of Art

Inspector Clink is working alone on this case. On important cases like this one he prefers to take charge of the whole investigation. But he is a little tired and hesitant now. Maybe he is getting too old for the job. The Inspector feels this may be his last case, and it is a difficult one. He knows he has a fifty-fifty chance of winning, no more than that...

editora ática

Inspector Clink is calling from a telephone box in London. He is speaking to a police informant. Now he has the information he needs. And he knows where he is going: Shakespeare Road, Bournemouth, in the south of England, about an hour and a half by train from London.

TELEPHONE
TEL

Kojak. Columbo. Magnum. Superstars! People watch the super policemen on TV and love their success stories. People think justice always wins. Well, I don't know. This is a difficult case. I have a fifty-fifty chance of success. No more than that.

Inspector Clink is on a train to Bournemouth. He is travelling alone. No police car, no detectives with him. He likes it that way. When the case is really important, he prefers to work alone. One or two telephone calls, and he has all the help he needs. But this time, something is different. Inspector Clink seems a little hesitant, a little uncertain. It's a hard case. A fifty-fifty chance of success, he thinks. But his destination is a secret, his mission is a secret. Everything is going to be O. K. Maybe he is getting old. And tired. Maybe this is his last case, who knows? The train is leaving. Inspector Clink is sleeping now.

This is a picture of Shakespeare Road, in Bournemouth. You can see Ashley's, the bookshop, at number 72. I know that bookshop and I know its owner, Mr. Ashley. I live in the same road, at number 43, but that's not important. I often go to Ashley's, but I don't buy anything there. You see, they specialize in art books, which are generally very expensive. Well, *for me* they are very expensive. I am just a teacher. I cannot buy those books. But I like to look at them. The pictures are so beautiful. That costs nothing...

BOOK SHOP
ASHLEY'S
ART BOOKS
ASHLEY'S
ART BOOKS
RESTAURANT

I often go to Ashley's, but there is one thing in that bookshop that I don't like: Mr. Ashley. I like it when he is not there, and that often happens. He is always travelling. They say he has business in London and several other cities in Europe. He is a rich man. He lives in an elegant Victorian villa near the sea, not far from Shakespeare Road. He comes to the bookshop in a very big car, he has a chauffeur, and there are always two big strong men with him. His "assistants". Of course Mr. Ashley is not Italian, he is British. But I look at him, his car, his bodyguards, and I remember Marlon Brando in *The Godfather*. Well, there they are! I'm not going to Ashley's today...

OP

There are not many people inside the bookshop now. Mr. Ashley is in his office, with his two "assistants". A lady is paying for some books and a man is talking to Mr. Moore, the manager. But wait a moment. We know that man. It's Inspector Clink! What is he doing here? He is saying something to the manager now. Something we cannot hear. What can it be?

Tell Mr. Ashley I want to talk to him.
Give him this book. Tell him to see page 24. There is a card too.
He can see my name there.
The name is Clink.
Inspector Clink, from Yard.

What is there on page 24 of that book?

A beautiful Picasso. A
lovely work of art. But
it is not in the museum
now. It's missing.
Inspector Clink.
Ireland Yard.
Do you have any idea
where it is?
GI
WITH A CAT
24

Tell the Inspector to come in, Mr. Moore.

MR ASHLEY

Please sit down, Inspector.
What can I do for you?

I suggest we have a *private*
conversation, Mr. Ashley.

Mr. Ashley's "assistants" are still in his office.

Mr. Ashley looks at the two bodyguards and tells them to leave the office. He says he does not need them now.

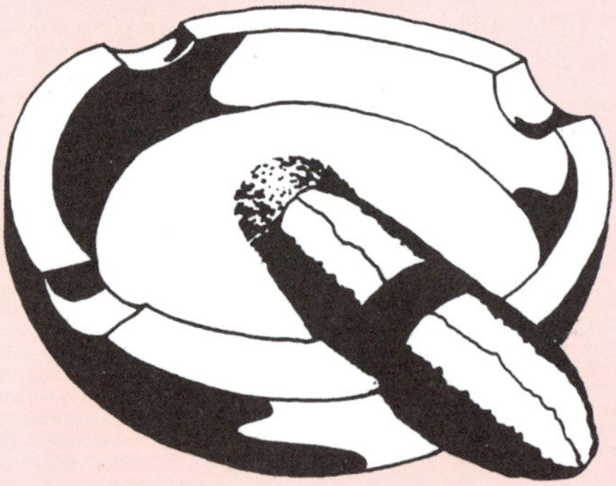

Suplemento de atividades

Shakespeare Road SERIES

A WORK OF ART

AMADEU MARQUES

editora ática

Inspector Clink is on his way to Bournemouth, a town on the south coast of England. He is not on vacation, far from it! He is working on an important investigation and he is travelling by himself. He likes it that way. When the case is really important, he prefers to work it alone. Another hard case, another secret mission, but this time something is different. Well, people say that justice always wins…

Elaboração do suplemento: Amini Rassoul, Leda de Aguiar Vieira.

Name____

Number________ Grade____________________________

School____

Language Activities

After you read the story, do these activities and HAVE FUN!

I *Circle the correct answers according to the story.*

1 Mr. Ashley lives
a in the south side of London.
b in an elegant Victorian villa.
c in Shakespeare Road.
d in his bookshop.

2 Mr. Ashley's shop specializes in
a works of art.
b school books.
c art books.
d all kinds of books.

3 The common fact about works of art is that
a they have no price.
b people never see them in museums.
c it is very difficult to steal them.
d they disappear from museums every year.

4 The owner of the bookshop
a has two bodyguards.
b comes from France.
c prefers to work with famous paintings.
d calls the Inspector in London.

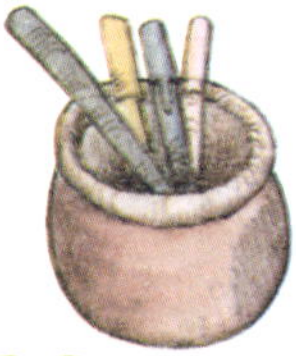

5 Inspector Clink can be characterized as
a a funny police officer.
b a nonviolent man.
c a generous investigator.
d a dishonest man.

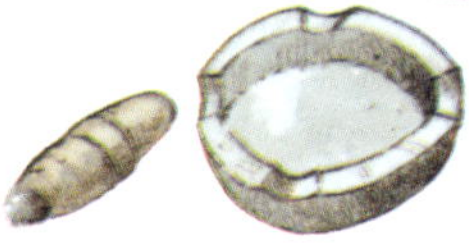

II Classify the statements below. Use **T** (True), **F** (False) or **NI** (No Information):

1 Inspector Clink lives with his wife. ( )
2 He thinks the case is hard to solve. ( )
3 He can't sleep on the train. ( )
4 Mr. Ashley works in England only. ( )
5 Inspector Clink works for Ireland Yard. ( )
6 Mr. Ashley's office has a bad alarm system. ( )

III What does the Inspector do before and after he arrives at Mr. Ashley's bookshop? Write **before** or **after** next to each statement.

Inspector Clink...

1 thinks about some famous TV policemen. ________
2 wants Mr. Ashley's "assistants" to leave the office. ________
3 calls a police informant from a telephone box in London. ________
4 opens his briefcase to show Picasso's painting to the bookshop owner. ________
5 asks the manager to give Mr. Ashley a book. ________

IV The statements below are based on the story. Say which are facts (F) and which are characters' opinions (O):

Examples: Justice always wins. **(** *O* **)**
Mr. Ashley is a rich man. **(** *F* **)**

1 The *Girl with a Cat* is a beautiful painting by Picasso. ( )
2 Inspector Clink puts the gun back in his pocket. ( )
3 Clink knows where the Picasso is. ( )

4 The police officer puts a lot of pressure on Mr. Ashley to give him some names. **( )**

5 The Inspector wants a million dollars for the painting. **( )**

6 Clink makes Mr. Ashley an excellent offer. **( )**

V *The story mentions some "occupations" people have. Fill in the missing letters to complete the occupations: (The* **first letter** *is given)*

1 Mr. Ashley does not drive his own car. He has a **c**__________.

2 Saudi Arabia is famous for its wealthy oil **s**__________.

3 A **r**__________ takes money or property illegally.

4 My godfather buys antiques because he is a **c**__________.

5 Mr. Ashley has an honest business. He is not a **c**__________.

VI *Find words from the story in the* **Word Search** *and complete the sentences:*

A	B	M	K	B	P	I	E	F	E
L	K	I	K	O	U	Y	S	Q	V
O	H	Q	W	D	X	Z	A	T	I
N	C	W	C	Y	H	J	C	P	S
E	N	O	U	G	H	V	F	M	N
Q	E	M	V	U	O	P	E	O	E
P	R	I	V	A	T	E	I	V	P
A	F	W	O	R	K	M	R	F	X
Y	U	L	M	D	K	H	B	R	E
X	V	W	L	S	O	U	T	H	K

1 The story is about a __________ of art.

2 Bournemouth is in the __________ of England.

3 On important cases, Inspector Clink prefers to work __________ .

4 Art books are generally __________ .

5 Mr. Ashley has two __________ .

6 Inspector Clink wants to have a __________ conversation with Mr. Ashley.

7 A small painting by Picasso is missing from the __________ Museum.

8 There are not __________ guards in museums.

9 The painting by Picasso is in the Inspector's __________ .

VII ***Fill in the chart with the missing words: the name of the country, the nationality and the name of the national language.***

COUNTRY	NATIONALITY	LANGUAGE
England	English	__________
__________	Italian	Italian
France	__________	French
Brazil	Brazilian	__________
Japan	__________	Japanese
Mexico	__________	Spanish
__________	Portuguese	Portuguese
The United States	__________	English

VIII *Circle the correct alternative to complete each sentence. The underlined words will help you:*

1 Inspector Clink is travelling by himself. That means he is travelling _________.

a on a train **b** alone **c** secretly

2 The Inspector looks a little uncertain. He is _________.

a hesitant **b** afraid **c** tired

3 Picasso's painting has an enormous value. It is very _________.

a inexpensive **b** limited **c** valuable

4 The Inspector is pointing a gun at Mr. Ashley. He is _________.

a successful **b** armed **c** rich

IX *Ask questions* **about** *Mr. Ashley:*

Example: *How does Mr. Ashley come to the bookshop?*
He comes to the bookshop by car.

1 ____

He lives in an elegant Victorian villa near the sea.

2 ____

He has two bodyguards.

3 ____

He sells art books.

X *Use* **indefinite pronouns** *to complete the sentences. The first one is done for you!*

1 Inspector Clink believes that **everything** is going to be OK.

2 The teacher doesn't buy ___________ at Ashley's.

3 The teacher just looks at the pictures. That costs ___________.

4 In the picture on page 10, Inspector Clink is saying ___________ to the manager.

5 Mr. Ashley says he knows ___________ about Picasso's painting.

6 The owner of the shop insists he doesn't know ___________ about the missing painting.

XI ***Choose the appropriate verb form in each sentence:***

1 Many people ___________ / **are liking** to watch policemen films on TV.

2 The Inspector thinks he ___________ / **gets** old.

3 The *Girl with a Cat* **misses** / ___________ from the French Museum.

4 The Ireland Yard **helps** / ___________ the French police and Interpol on the case.

5 Mr. Ashley ___________ / **is having** connections in the art world.

XII ***Complete the sentences with* prepositions*. The pages where you can find them are shown in parentheses:***

1 **(p. 2)** We have to stop this conversation now. I'm calling _______ my mobile phone.

2 **(p. 2)** Please don't interrupt me. I'm speaking _______ your mother.

3 **(p. 6)** We live _______ number 637, Heathrow Road.

4 **(p. 8)** Look _______ that pretty painting on the wall!

5 **(p. 18)** Those people have serious problems and they are asking _______ help.

6 **(p. 18)** Sorry, but I have no idea of what you are talking _______!

Don't you think that* A Work of Art *has a surprising end? How would* you *continue the story? Choose another ending to the story from the alternatives below:

1 Mr. Ashley is a real robber and goes to prison.

2 Mr. Ashley is a policeman and takes Inspector Clink to prison.

3 Inspector Clink has a heart attack and dies in Mr. Ashley's office.

4 Mr. Ashley's "assistants" come into his office and steal the painting.

5 Mr. Ashley and Inspector Clink become good friends.

6 Mr. Ashley fights with the Inspector and knocks him down.

7 The police arrive and take both the Inspector and Mr. Ashley to prison.

8 The painting that the Inspector has is fake (= not genuine).

9 The bookshop manager comes in and accepts the Inspector's offer.

10 The Inspector sells Mr. Ashley the painting and buys his bookshop.

"Now we can talk," says the Inspector. "Mr. Ashley, you know that the *Girl with a cat*, the small painting by Picasso, is missing from the French Museum. It is difficult to say the total value of the artworks that disappear from museums every year. But it's enormous. That is a criminal activity that involves millions and millions of dollars. Those paintings simply disappear. We never see them again. The Ireland Yard is co-operating with the French police and the Interpol on this case."

"But Inspector," says Mr. Ashley. "I don't see why you're telling me all that. I know nothing about that painting."

"Don't worry, this is not an interrogation," says the Inspector. "I am just asking for your help. We know that you can help us. It is not very difficult to steal a painting from one of those museums. Not enough guards, bad alarm systems. The robbers know all about it. The difficult part comes after that. Where can a robber sell a Picasso from the French Museum? That's when your participation is important, Mr. Ashley. You have good connections in the art world and you can find a client for the Picasso. In return for your information and help, the French authorities are offering you..."

Mr. Ashley interrupts the Inspector now. "I don't know what you are talking about," he says. "I have an honest occupation. An honest business. I am not a criminal!"

Names, Mr. Ashley, names. Just give me the names. O.K., you don't know anything about the Picasso. But you have your contacts. That is a big help to me. That work of art has no price. The French want it back and I am not going back to London with no names, Mr. Ashley.

Mr. Ashley is standing now. For him, that is the end of the conversation.

Now Inspector Clink has a gun in his hand. And he is pointing it at Mr. Ashley.

"I need those names," the Inspector says. "Who are the robbers? Who are your contacts? My informants tell me that you receive the paintings and then find a client for them. A Japanese millionaire, or an oil sheik from Saudi Arabia. Or a crazy collector who pays a fortune for a painting that only *he* can see. That market is very limited. We know about your importance in it. We have information that you work on a fifty-fifty basis. You get 50 percent of the profits. We know all about you. But I just want you to give me the names, especially the names of the robbers. Who steals the paintings and then brings them to you? Tell me now, Mr. Ashley. I don't want to kill you. Do you understand?"

Mr. Ashley, white with terror, does not say anything. He just looks at the Inspector. It seems that he cannot speak.

Names! My name is Ashley. That's all I know!
All right. This is the end of the test. I'm satisfied.

Inspector Clink puts the gun back in his pocket and sits down. A smile comes to his face.

I know where the Picasso is. It's here, in my briefcase. It's a small painting, but it has enormous value.

Two million dollars. Give me one million and it's all yours. Fifty-fifty, right?

about: sobre, a respeito de; cerca de, mais ou menos
activity: atividade
after: depois de
again: novamente
alone: sozinho
always: sempre

artwork: obra de arte
to ask for: pedir
authorities: autoridades
back: de volta
bad: mau, ruim

beautiful: belo
beginning: começo
bodyguard: guarda-costas
bookshop: livraria (G.B., = bookstore, E.U.A.)

briefcase: pasta (para documentos etc.)
to bring: trazer
British: britânico
business: negócio(s)
to buy: comprar
call: ligação
card: cartão

cat: gato
chauffeur: chofer
cheap: barato
cities: cidades
collector: colecionador
to come: vir; chegar
to come in: entrar
connection: ligação, conexão
conversation: conversa
to cost: custar

crazy: maluco
criminal: criminoso
destination: destino (para onde se vai)
to disappear: desaparecer
end: fim, final
enough: suficiente(s)
especially: principalmente
everything: tudo
expensive: caro
face: rosto
far (from): longe (de)
fifty-fifty: meio a meio
to find: achar, encontrar

fortune: fortuna
French: francês
from: (vindo) de

generally: geralmente
to get: pegar; receber
to get old: ficar velho
to give: dar
godfather: padrinho
gun: arma de fogo
half: metade; meio
hand: mão
to happen: acontecer
hard: duro; difícil

to hear: ouvir
here: aqui
hesitant: hesitante, indeciso
inside: dentro (de)
interrogation: interrogatório
to involve: envolver
Ireland Yard: instituição fictícia, referência humorística à Scotland Yard, a polícia britânica
just: só, apenas
to kill: matar
lady: senhora
last: último
to leave: deixar, sair (de)
little: pequeno; pouco
a little: um pouco, um tanto
to look at: olhar para
lovely: lindo, adorável
manager: gerente
maybe: talvez
missing: desaparecido
mission: missão
near: perto (de)
of course: é claro, naturalmente
to offer: oferecer

office: escritório
often: freqüentemente

oil sheik: xeque do petróleo
only: apenas
other: outro(s)
owner: dono
page: página
painting: pintura, quadro
to pay (for): pagar
pocket: bolso
to point at: apontar para
price: preço
private: particular
profit: lucro
to put: pôr, colocar
to receive: receber
to return: retornar
in return for: em troca de

rich: rico
right: certo; direito

robber: ladrão
same: mesmo, igual
satisfied: satisfeito
to say: dizer
they say: dizem que
sea: mar
secret: segredo, secreto
to see: ver

to seem: parecer
to sell: vender
several: diversos, vários
simply: simplesmente
to sit down: sentar(-se)

to sleep: dormir
small: pequeno
smile: sorriso
so: tão
sorry: triste, pesaroso
I'm sorry: sinto muito

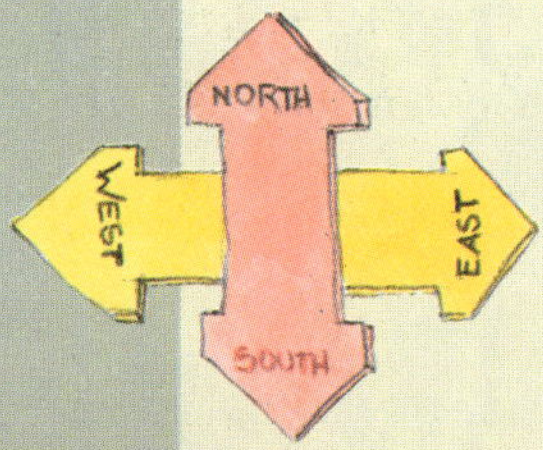

south: sul
standing: de pé
to steal: roubar
still: ainda
strong: forte
to suggest: sugerir
to talk (to): falar (com)
to tell: dizer, contar (a)
terribly: terrivelmente
then: então
there: lá
there they are!: lá estão eles!
tired: cansado
too: também

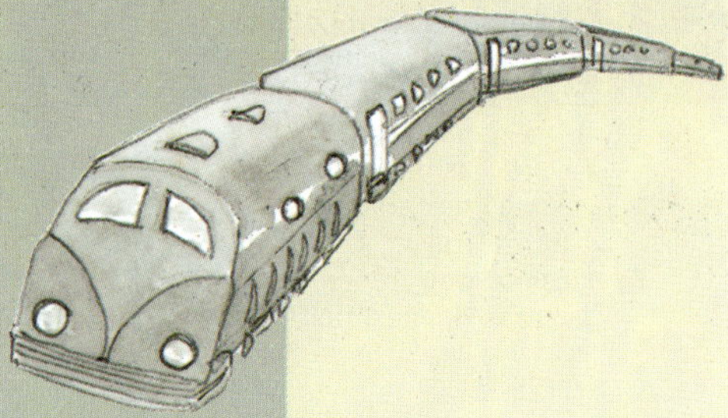

train: trem
to travel: viajar
uncertain: incerto, inseguro
to understand: compreender
value: valor
Victorian: vitoriano (estilo arquitetônico inglês)
villa: casa grande e rica
to wait: esperar
to want: querer
way: modo, maneira
that way: assim
which: que, o qual, os quais
white: branco
who: quem

to win: vencer
work of art: obra de arte
to worry: preocupar-se
Yard: abreviação de Ireland/Scotland Yard